THE CONSTELLATION PEGASUS

STACY ALLEN

childsworld.com

Published by The Child's World®
800-599-READ • www.childsworld.com

Photography Credits
Photographs ©: Shutterstock Images, cover (illustration), cover (background), 1 (illustration), 1 (background), 2 (illustration), 2–3, 7 (illustration), 13; E. Slawik/NSF/AURA/M. Zamani/NOIRLab, cover (constellation), 1 (constellation), 2 (constellation), 7 (constellation), 27; NASA, 5, 11; NSF/AURA/NOIRLab, 9; KPNO/NSF/AURA/Paul Mortfield and Dietmar Kupke/Flynn Haase/NOIRLab, 10; Marie-Lan Nguyen/Townley Collection/British Museum, 14; Fah Ozzy/Shutterstock Images, 17; Matt LaVigne/Shutterstock Images, 19; Fine Art Images/Heritage Images/Hulton Archive/Getty Images, 20; Michele Vacchiano/Shutterstock Images, 22; piemags/Alamy, 23; Erik Cornelius/Nationalmuseum, 25; fdecomite/Flickr, 29; Design elements from Shutterstock Images

ISBN Information
9781503875821 (Reinforced Library Binding)
9781503876248 (Portable Document Format)
9781503876866 (Online Multi-user eBook)
9781503877368 (Electronic Publication)

LCCN 2025938267

Printed in the United States of America

ABOUT THE AUTHOR

Stacy Allen learned to navigate by the stars when she sailed on board the schooner R/V *Westward* in the Atlantic Ocean and Caribbean Sea. She lives with her family in Maryland and loves to look for constellations and deep-sky objects at night.

TABLE OF CONTENTS

CHAPTER ONE

The Constellation Pegasus

A winged horse flies above Earth every night. This horse is made of stars. His body is a huge square in the sky. This is the constellation Pegasus. Pegasus was a flying horse in Greek **mythology**. He helped heroes and gods. Pegasus earned a special place among the stars. In the Northern **Hemisphere**, the whole constellation appears to be upside down.

Pegasus is the seventh-largest constellation. A constellation is a group of stars that makes a picture in the night sky. It takes some imagination to look at the stars and see pictures. But humans have looked for patterns in the stars since **ancient** times. Constellations help people measure time and find their way. Many cultures have stories about their constellations. Modern **astronomers** recognize 88 official constellations.

Stars are hot balls of burning gas. The stars visible from Earth are part of the Milky Way **galaxy**. This is Earth's galaxy. The Milky Way has at least 100,000,000,000 (100 billion) stars. On a very dark night, a person on Earth can see about 5,000 stars.

Earth's Sun is a star. The Sun is so bright that during the daytime, other stars are not usually visible. But Earth's Sun is not the brightest star. It only appears so bright because it is the closest star to Earth.

The Sun appears larger than other stars because it is closer to Earth than other stars. But there are stars 100 times larger than the Sun.

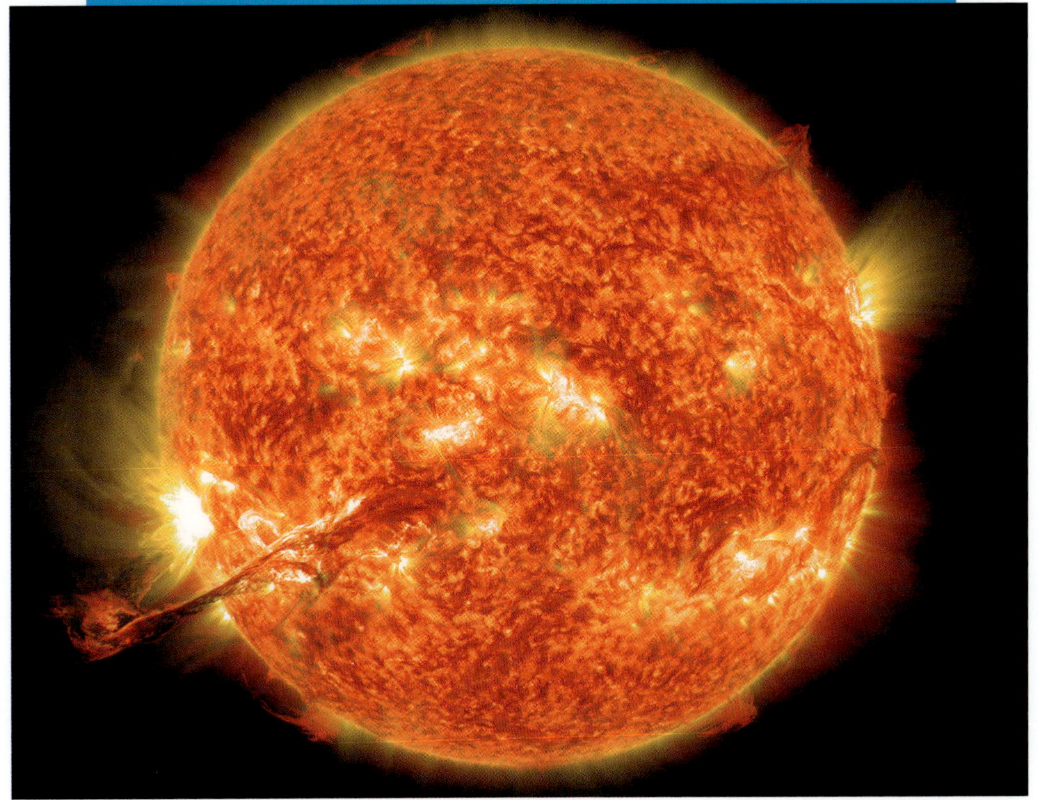

The four bright stars that make up the main body of Pegasus are known as the Great Square of Pegasus. This square is called an asterism. An asterism is an easily recognizable shape that is not an official constellation. The Great Square is Pegasus's body. The star Markab marks where Pegasus's neck meets the square of his body. The star Scheat marks where his front legs meet the square. Pegasus's hind legs and tail are not included in the constellation. But the star leading to where Pegasus's tail would begin is named Algenib.

Alpheratz is the fourth star in the Great Square. But this star is not actually part of Pegasus. It belongs to Andromeda, a neighboring constellation. Throughout history, astronomers disagreed on where Alpheratz belonged. Some placed the star in Pegasus. *Alpheratz* means "the horse's navel" in Arabic. But others placed the star in Andromeda. The International Astronomical Union (IAU) is the organization that determined the official constellations. In the 1930s, the IAU placed Alpheratz in Andromeda. So Alpheratz is not officially part of the Pegasus constellation. But it does finish up the Great Square of Pegasus's body.

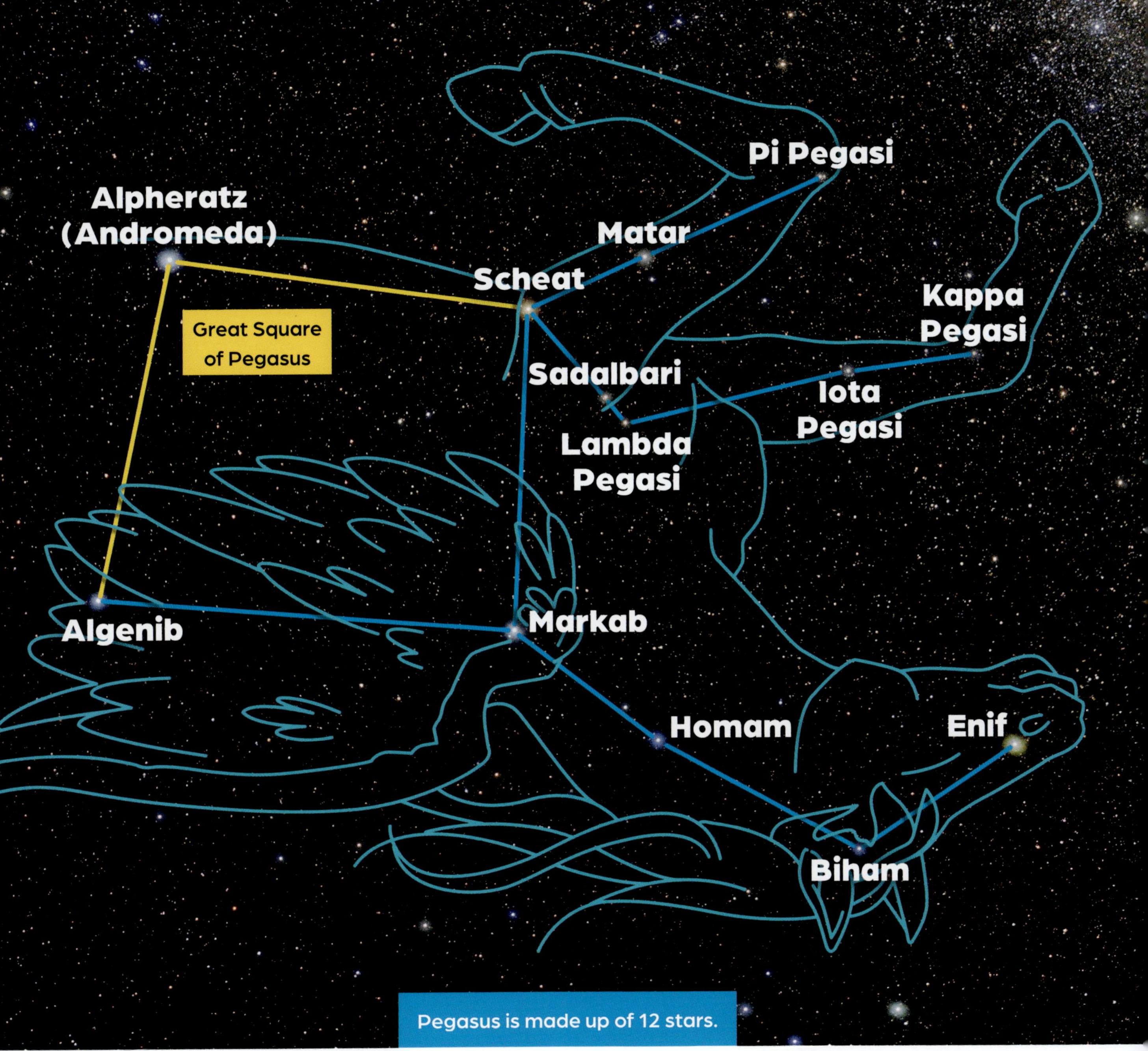

Pegasus is made up of 12 stars.

Pegasus is more than the Great Square. The brightest star in Pegasus is its nose. This is the star Enif. Biham marks the top of the head. Sadalbari and Matar are part of Pegasus's front legs.

The area of sky around a constellation is considered part of that constellation. Pegasus contains more than just stars. There are also deep-sky objects. These objects include star clusters and galaxies. A star cluster is a group of stars that were born together. Pegasus also contains planets. In 1995, astronomers discovered the first planet **orbiting** a star similar to Earth's Sun. The star was 51 Pegasi. Scientists now know that many stars have planets in orbit. Pegasus has at least 11 planets orbiting its stars.

EVERYTHING IN MOTION

Stars seem to move across the night sky because Earth is spinning on its axis. Earth also orbits the Sun. The whole solar system is located on one arm of the spiral Milky Way galaxy. The Milky Way is just one galaxy spinning in the vast universe. The universe contains hundreds of billions of galaxies in motion. And the universe is growing and expanding.

Just beyond Enif at the nose of Pegasus is a special globular cluster. This is a bright, dense group of more than 100,000 stars. Its name is Messier 15 (M15). M15 is one of the densest star clusters in the Milky Way. It appears very bright in the dark space near the star Enif. Scientists believe M15 may have a **black hole** at its core.

M15 is a tightly packed cluster.

Two groups of galaxies can be seen near the Great Square of Pegasus. The first one is called the Deer Lick Group. One galaxy in this group has been called the Milky Way's twin. This is because galaxy NGC 7331 and the Milky Way are similar in shape and size.

NGC 7331 is similar to Earth's galaxy, the Milky Way.

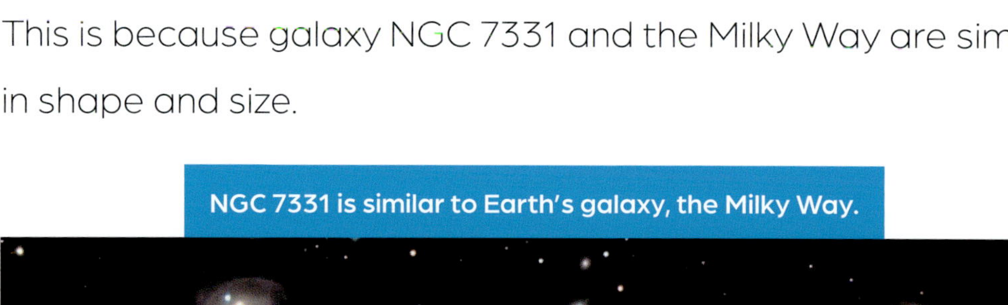

Édouard Stephan was a French astronomer. He discovered Stephan's Quintet in 1877.

Another galaxy group in Pegasus is Stephan's Quintet. It includes five galaxies that seem clustered together. Four of these galaxies are very near each other. The other is much closer to the Milky Way than the other four.

CHAPTER TWO

The Origin of the Myth

Ancient Mesopotamians drew the constellation that became Pegasus. Mesopotamians lived in what is now the Middle East. They created many constellations. They first saw the Great Square as a horse more than 3,000 years ago.

Astronomers in ancient Greece saw the horse constellation, too. Pegasus was the most famous horse in Greek mythology. He was born of Poseidon and Medusa. Poseidon was the Greek god of the sea. He was also the god of horses. Medusa was a monster called a Gorgon. These terrifying winged monsters have snakes for hair. The hero Bellerophon was able to tame and ride Pegasus. But Bellerophon made the gods angry. Zeus punished Bellerophon but honored Pegasus by making him a constellation.

In some stories, Bellerophon was also Poseidon's son. That would mean Pegasus and Bellerophon were brothers.

HOMER

Homer is the author of the *Iliad* and the *Odyssey*. The *Iliad* is about the Trojan War. The *Odyssey* is about a soldier named Odysseus and his journey home from the war. Historians do not know much about Homer. He may have been a real poet. Or "Homer" may be a name given to many poets who told these stories over time.

Stories of the Greek gods and heroes were told aloud by poets. Homer was a famous poet in ancient Greece. More than 2,500 years ago, Homer told the story of Bellerophon in his famous poem the *Iliad*.

Ptolemy (TAH-luh-mee) was a Greco-Roman astronomer. In about AD 150, Ptolemy wrote about 48 constellations. He continued the work of many earlier astronomers. Most of these constellations are included in the 88 modern constellations. Ptolemy kept the horse constellation. He knew the Greek legends of the horse with wings. In his star catalog, Ptolemy named the constellation "Pegasus."

CHAPTER THREE

The Story of Pegasus

Long ago, Poseidon fell in love with a woman named Medusa. Medusa was known for her beauty, especially her beautiful hair. Poseidon met with Medusa in the temple of the goddess Athena. This made Athena angry. She decided to punish Medusa. Athena turned Medusa into a Gorgon, a terrifying monster. She transformed Medusa's beautiful hair into **venomous** snakes. One look at the monster would turn any human into stone. Medusa went to live with the other Gorgons at the edge of the world.

The young hero Perseus was sent on a quest to defeat Medusa. It was meant to be impossible. A king had fallen in love with Perseus's mother. He ordered Perseus to bring him Medusa's head. He hoped to get Perseus out of the way with this difficult task.

Medusa was the only Gorgon who could be killed.

But Perseus had help from the gods. Athena and Hermes gave Perseus tools to help in his quest. A cap made him invisible. Winged sandals helped him travel. The gods gave him a sickle, or a curved blade, to cut off Medusa's head. They also gave him a bag to carry the head.

Perseus arrived at the Gorgons' home. He knew he had to be careful. If Medusa looked at him, he would be turned into stone. Perseus used his shield like a mirror. He used its reflection to find Medusa without looking directly at her. Then he cut off her head. Two creatures came out of Medusa's neck. One was the giant Chrysaor (krih-SAWR). Some stories say he was a winged **boar**. The other was Pegasus. He was a beautiful white horse with wings.

PERSEUS'S STORY

Perseus took Medusa's head and used it to rescue Princess Andromeda. Andromeda was the daughter of Queen Cassiopeia and King Cepheus. She was being attacked by a sea monster. But Perseus killed the monster. When an army tried to stop his and Andromeda's wedding, Perseus used Medusa's head to turn the attackers to stone. This story is remembered in the stars. The Perseus Family of constellations includes King Cepheus, Queen Cassiopeia, Andromeda, and Pegasus. In some later versions of the story, Perseus rides Pegasus when he defeats the sea monster.

Bellerophon used a golden bridle from Athena to tame Pegasus.

Stories began to spread about Pegasus. A young man named Bellerophon heard that people had seen a horse with wings. He was fascinated with the stories.

Bellerophon loved horses. One day, Bellerophon found Pegasus. But Pegasus flew away whenever Bellerophon got too close. Bellerophon longed to ride Pegasus. He prayed to Athena for help. Athena gave Bellerophon a magic golden **bridle**. Bellerophon found Pegasus drinking from a fountain. He used the bridle, and Pegasus began to trust him. He even allowed Bellerophon to climb onto his back and fly!

King Iobates (eye-OH-buh-deez) of Lycia asked Bellerophon for help. There was a fierce monster destroying villages. It was called the Chimera (kye-MEER-uh). The Chimera had the head of a powerful lion. At her tail was a venomous snake's head. In the middle of her back was the head of a goat. The Chimera attacked people and animals. She could even breathe fire! Bellerophon knew he could not get close enough to defeat the Chimera with a sword. He had a special long spear made. The spear's tip was made of a soft metal called lead.

The word *chimera* is used today to mean a fantasy or something made up.

Bellerophon and Pegasus worked together to defeat the Chimera.

Bellerophon and Pegasus flew to a town where the Chimera was burning homes and killing everything in her path. They swooped in from above. The Chimera blew great balls of fire at them. Her animal heads tried to trap and bite them. But Bellerophon and Pegasus escaped. The next time the Chimera breathed fire, Pegasus flew down as close as he could. Bellerophon plunged the spear into the monster's throat. The soft metal melted, and the Chimera choked. Bellerophon and Pegasus won the battle!

King Iobates sent Bellerophon and Pegasus to defeat many more enemies of the kingdom. Eventually, Bellerophon married the king's daughter. But he still wanted more. Bellerophon believed he deserved to live on Mount Olympus. This was the home of the gods. One day he decided to take Pegasus and fly to the mountain's top.

Zeus was the king of the gods. He looked out from Olympus and saw Bellerophon coming. This made Zeus angry. He sent a horsefly to sting Pegasus. Pegasus bucked in pain. Bellerophon was thrown off the horse and fell through the sky, all the way back to Earth. He was badly injured. But Pegasus continued to fly. He made it to the top of Mount Olympus. Pegasus was welcomed by the gods.

For the rest of his days, Pegasus lived on Mount Olympus. He carried lightning bolts and thunder for Zeus. When Pegasus died, Zeus placed him among the stars as a constellation.

Bellerophon fell from Pegasus's back while trying to reach Mount Olympus.

CHAPTER FOUR

The Myth of Pegasus in Other Cultures

The Greek stories of constellations are some of the most well known. But many cultures around the world saw patterns in the night sky. They created different constellations from their own stories and traditions.

In North America, Native Americans have studied the movement of stars and planets. Planet and star locations helped people know when to plant and harvest food. They also helped for planning travel. Lakota stargazers looked at the Great Square and drew *Keya*, the Great Turtle. The turtle is a sacred animal for the Lakota. It represents Mother Earth. Her shell is the Great Square asterism in the sky. Ojibwe stargazers see the Great Square as the body of *Mooz*, the Moose. The constellation Lacerta is the moose's antler.

Chinese astronomers created different shapes from Pegasus's stars. Markab and Scheat formed an emperor's palace. Algenib and Alpheratz made a wall or a library. Other stars in Pegasus created a rooftop and a mortar and pestle for grinding food.

Mooz has stars from Pisces the Fish, Pegasus, and Lacerta the Lizard.

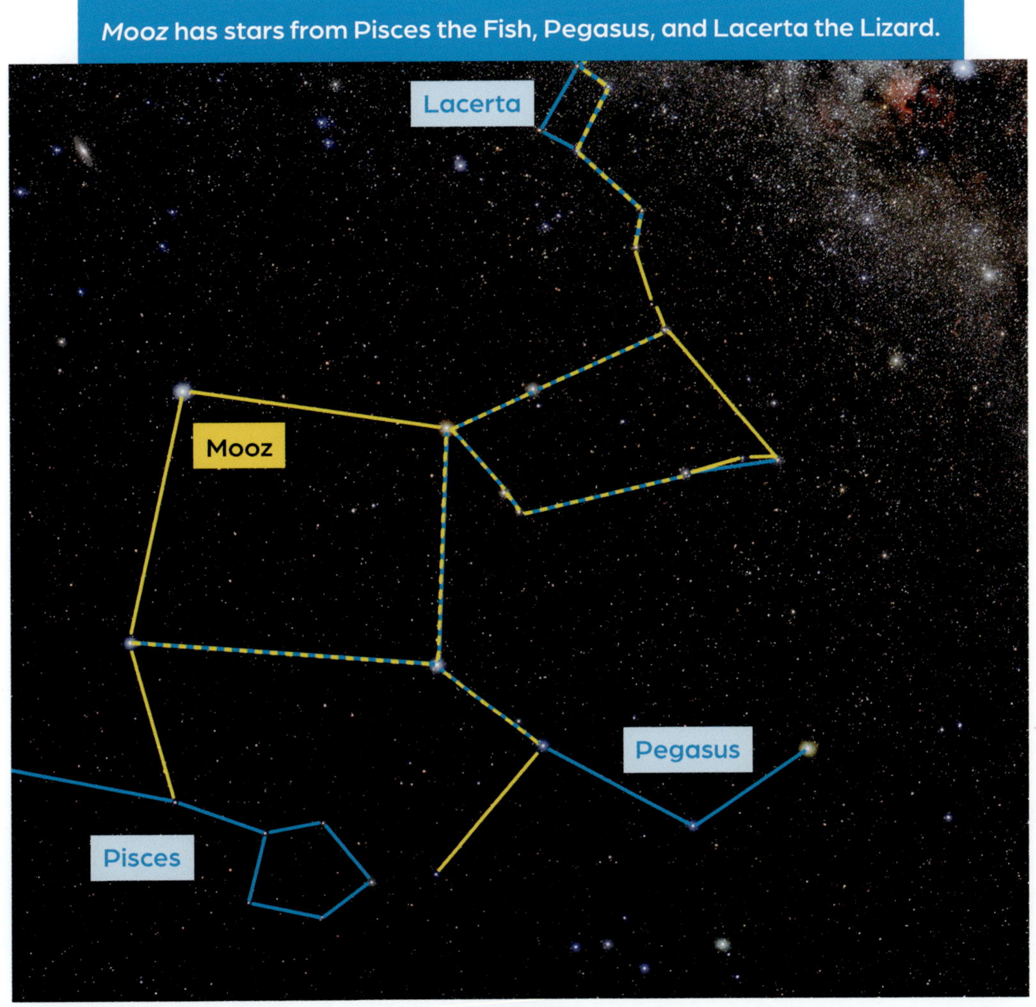

CHAPTER FIVE

How to Find Pegasus in the Sky

Autumn is the best time to view Pegasus in the Northern Hemisphere. In October, Pegasus rises to its highest point in the night sky. This is the best time to view the whole constellation. Look for the four bright stars of the Great Square. Then look for Pegasus's head and legs. Remember Pegasus will be upside down. Look for bright Enif at his nose.

In the Southern Hemisphere, it is easiest to spot Pegasus in spring. Look to the northern sky in October. Pegasus will be flying right side up.

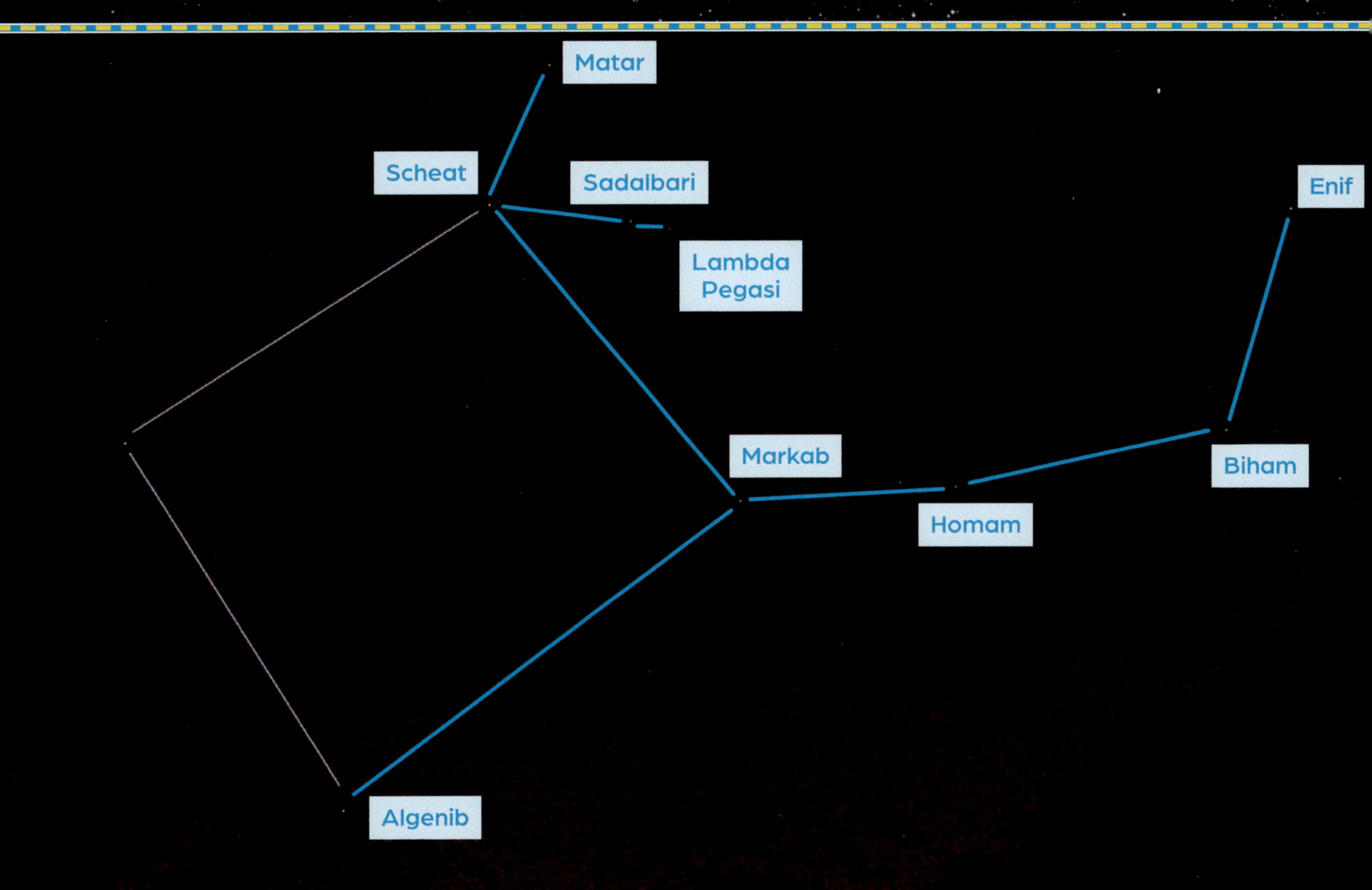

It may be difficult to see all the stars in a constellation's outline. But the brightest stars can help stargazers find the general shape.

GLOSSARY

ancient (AYN-shunt) Something that is ancient is very old or belongs to times long ago. Ancient Greeks told stories about Pegasus and Bellerophon.

astronomers (uh-STRAW-nuh-murz) Astronomers are scientists who study stars and other objects in space. Astronomers disagreed on whether Alpheratz belonged in Pegasus or Andromeda.

black hole (BLAK HOHL) A black hole is a space object caused by the collapse of a very large star. Astronomers think there may be a black hole at the center of M15.

boar (BORE) A boar is a male pig. In some stories, Pegasus's brother Chrysaor is a boar with wings.

bridle (BRYE-dull) A bridle is a set of straps and reins that go onto a horse's head to give a rider control. Athena gave Bellerophon a golden bridle to help him tame and ride Pegasus.

galaxy (GAL-uhk-see) A galaxy is a group of dust, gases, and billions of stars held together by gravity. Earth's galaxy is called the Milky Way.

hemisphere (HEH-mih-sfeer) A hemisphere is half of a sphere. Earth is divided into the Northern Hemisphere and Southern Hemisphere.

mythology (mih-THAW-luh-jee) Mythology is a culture's set of stories or beliefs. In Greek mythology, Pegasus carried lightning bolts for the god Zeus.

orbiting (OR-bih-ting) When an object is orbiting another object, it takes a rounded path around it. Astronomers found planets orbiting stars in Pegasus.

universe (YOO-nih-vers) The universe is everything that exists in space. Stars, galaxies, and other objects make up the universe.

venomous (VEN-uh-mus) Something venomous can cause injury by biting or stinging with a toxic substance called venom. Medusa had venomous snakes on her head instead of hair.

FAST FACTS

- Constellations are groupings of stars in the sky that form pictures. Stars are glowing balls of gas throughout the universe. The Sun is a star.
- Pegasus is the seventh-largest of the 88 official constellations. Pegasus is a winged horse. Its body is created by the Great Square asterism.
- Enif is the brightest star in the Pegasus constellation.
- The constellation Pegasus contains many deep-sky objects, including galaxies and star clusters.
- Pegasus was a winged horse in ancient Greek stories. He helped the hero Bellerophon with heroic deeds. Later on, he carried lightning bolts for Zeus.
- Lakota stargazers see Pegasus as a turtle. Ojibwe stargazers see a moose.
- In the Northern Hemisphere, the constellation Pegasus appears upside down. It is most easily seen in the fall.

ONE STRIDE FURTHER

- Look at the stars that create Pegasus. Would you create a different shape out of them? What would it be? Tell the story of your new constellation.
- The goddess Athena gave Bellerophon a magic bridle to help tame Pegasus. Would you have used this gift? Or would you want Pegasus to stay wild and free?
- Imagine you have discovered a new galaxy with billions of stars. What would you name it? Why?

FIND OUT MORE

IN THE LIBRARY

de la Bedoyere, Camilla. *My First Guide to Space*. Somerville, MA: Candlewick Press, 2024.

Owings, Lisa. *The Constellation Cassiopeia*. Parker, CO: The Child's World, 2026.

Tracosas, L. J. *Ultimate Greek Mythology*. New York, NY: Z Kids, 2023.

ON THE WEB

Visit our website for links about Pegasus:

childsworld.com/links

Note to Parents, Caregivers, Teachers, and Librarians: We routinely verify our web links to make sure they are safe and active sites. So encourage your readers to check them out!

INDEX